Sports Day
Snack Attack

Chapters		Page
1	Exciting News	4
2	No Cheating!	10
3	Fangtastic Football	18
4	Snack Attack	24

Written by Sheryl Webster
Illustrated by Pete Williamson

The Fang Family

Father Fang

Mother Fang

Grandpa Fang

Small Fang

Baby Fang

Veino

Did you know?

Vampires …
- have red eyes and fangs.
- hate light.
- love the taste of blood.
- can change into bats.

Funny Fang Family Fact:

Mother and Father Fang feel proud when they see Small Fang scaring other children.

1

Exciting News

Slop! Squelch! Mother Fang smeared factor 100 sun cream onto Small Fang.

"There! Now you can go out without worrying."

It was Small Fang's first day at school. He was very excited!

At the school gates, Mother and Father Fang watched Small Fang chasing the other children.

"I am so proud," said Mother Fang, smiling.

The bell rang and Small Fang pushed to get to the front of the line. Quick as a wink, out came the bat wings, and *whoosh!*

They all sat down at their tables in the classroom. Miss Wobble had some exciting news.

She held up a poster.

"We will practise today," she said. "You can each do one event. Your mother or father may take part with you."

"I wonder what I'll be picked for," thought Small Fang.

2
No Cheating!

First, they tried the egg and spoon race. Small Fang really wanted to be picked for this, so he held up his claws.

"Raaaaah!"

he roared.

The other children were so frightened that they dropped their eggs. Small Fang was pleased. Miss Wobble was not.

"Perhaps you should try the sack race," said Miss Wobble.

Small Fang grinned. He just knew he would be good at this. As he hopped, he glared at the other children with his blazing red eyes.

"Help!" they shouted and fell all over each other.

"Well," said Miss Wobble. "It seems we can't put you in the sack race either!" She sighed and sent him over to the high jump.

"This is easy!" said Small Fang as he *flew* over the pole.

"Now *that's* just cheating!" said Miss Wobble.

The football coach came over. "You're fast!" he said. "Would you like to play for the mini-football team?"

"Yes, please! Fangks!" said Small Fang. He was thrilled. So was Miss Wobble. After all, what trouble could he get into playing football?

Fangtastic Football

After school Mother Fang was waiting at the gates.

"How was your day?" she asked.

"Great!" said Small Fang. "The football coach thinks I'm fangtastic. I'm not sure the other children do. When I smile at them, they run away."

"But you have such a lovely smile!" said Mother Fang.

Small Fang couldn't wait to tell Father Fang his news.

"You and me, Dad, in the school football team!"

Father Fang bought a ball to practise with ...

then another ...

and another.

"I don't understand why they keep going flat," said Father Fang. He soon discovered that Grandpa was to blame.

Now Father Fang and Small Fang had a new ball and no Grandpa. They began to practise hard.

They learned how to dribble the ball.

They learned how to head the ball.

They learned
how to tackle
each other.

And they shot fangtastic goals
between the goal ghosts.

4

Snack Attack

Saturday came and Small Fang trotted onto the pitch with Father Fang. Mother Fang, Baby Fang and Grandpa Fang cheered from the sidelines.

Father Fang raced down the pitch. He passed the ball to Small Fang and …

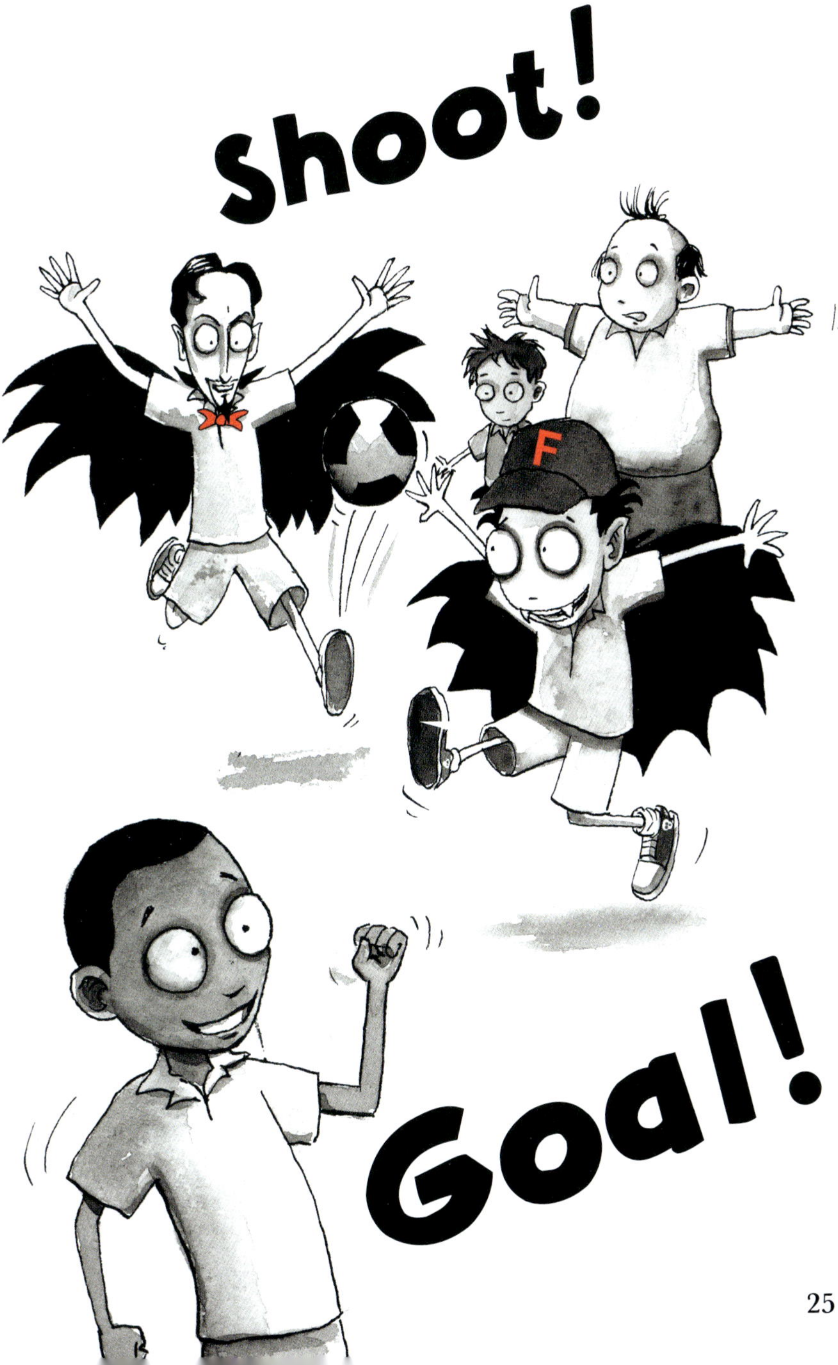
Shoot!
Goal!

Father Fang and Small Fang were the stars of their team. Goal after goal shot into the net.

The crowd went wild. "Small Fang! Small Fang!" they chanted.

"They all love you now!" shouted Mother Fang.

Suddenly, someone got hurt. Blood trickled down his leg.

Small Fang stopped and his red eyes glazed over. He licked his lips.

"Yummy!" he shouted. "Lunch time!"

"No feeding on your friends!"
shouted Father Fang.

But it was too late. Small Fang was already running towards the player. The frightened player struggled up and limped away as fast as he could. The crowd screamed and ran.

Father Fang tried to say sorry to Miss Wobble, but she ran away too.

Back at home, Mother Fang sighed. "Never mind, we'll find you a new school."

"One where you can play football," added Father Fang.

"Oh, I don't want to *play* football now," grinned Small Fang. "I want to be the team's first aid person!"